lessons in balance

lessons in balance:

A DOG'S REFLECTIONS ON LIFE

by Scout

RUNNING PRESS
PHILADELPHIA · LONDON

The Author will donate a portion of her royalties from
this book to various charities that care for animals.

Books published by Running Press are available at special discounts for bulk purchases in the United States by corporations, institutions, and other organizations. For more information, please contact the Special Markets Department at the Perseus Books Group, 2300 Chestnut Street, Suite 200, Philadelphia, PA 19103, or call (800) 810-4145, ext. 5000, or e-mail special.markets@perseusbooks.com.

ISBN 978-0-7624-5524-9
Library of Congress Control Number: 2014939506

E-book ISBN 978-0-7624-5551-5
9 8 7 6 5 4 3 2 1
Digit on the right indicates the number of this printing

Cover design by Sarah Hoy
Interior design by Sarah Hoy
Edited by Sophia Muthuraj
Typography: ITC Century, New Century Schoolbook,Trade Gothic Condensed
Photography by Madi Chambers of East Lake Photography,
Christian Webber, and N. Maxwell Lander

Running Press Book Publishers
2300 Chestnut Street
Philadelphia, PA 19103-4371

Visit us on the web!
www.runningpress.com

To all the dogs waiting to be rescued
by their own human, to show them
just how amazing they are.

———————————————

I t all started when a friend and I noticed how flat Scout's head was; being a pit bull, he exhibits the characteristic square/flat head. So on a whim, I placed one roll of toilet paper on his head, and to my amazement he stood motionless, not unlike a statue, and balanced it perfectly. From then on, he showed a knack for balancing almost anything I put on his head: a single strawberry, a netbook, burgers, sushi, wigs—and that was just the beginning. As I shared his unique skill on my personal blog, I quickly realized how much joy Scout brought to people. The blog, *Stuff on Scout's Head,* also became a perfect platform to show people how patient, loyal, smart, and loving pit bulls really can be with the right type of training.

There is no better example than Scout himself. When I first got Scout from a rescue, he was an entirely different dog. He was gaunt, antisocial, and scared. I don't know his history, but I assume he was no stranger to the pound. Once he was rescued, he had to be separated from the other dogs, since he was so fearful of them. When I heard about him, I knew I had to get him. I was the first person he didn't greet by jumping on nervously. I wanted to help him; I could see the potential in his eyes. American Pit Bull Terriers are such a misunderstood breed, but I love them. I had no shortage of love for this shy pit bull and was determined to transform him and bring him out of his shell. It was also great that my friends and their dogs were committed to helping Scout. It seemed like a perfect fit.

At first when I brought him into my home, he didn't play with any toys that I had for him, and he timidly grazed at his food and hated cuddling. It was obvious that he had been given up on, neglected, mistreated; he was so unfamiliar with these things that are staples in any dog's life. I can't imagine how someone so dear to me now was once treated with such carelessness. As any pet owner knows, it's hard to quantify how much your pet means to you or when exactly a pet becomes a part of the family; but for me, all of this was immediate. Scout was slow to trust me but when he did, he started to blossom.

People say that dogs live in the present and that's very true of Scout. When I bring out an object, he offers the spot on his head where we usually balance the object, sits, and freezes when it is placed. Nothing else matters to him at that moment; his concentration is unbreakable. Of course, he couldn't possibly be more delighted to receive treats afterward. I'm amazed time after time by his doggy mindfulness and his Zen-like ability to balance literally anything.

I'm glad to say that with his popular blog and now with this book, Scout hopes to share his message of mindfulness and balance with people all over the world. He is also a perfect ambassador for why pit bulls can make amazing pets, and I couldn't be prouder of him. We have become incredible partners in crime, and to me he is not only an Internet star and author but a companion with character and personality. We've learned a lot from each other. From me he's learned to trust and love, and from him I've learned to be present and mindful, focus on the task at hand, and complete it. Just breathe in and breathe out. As you will see in this book, the other thing we've both learned while trying to live a well-balanced life is that you can't take yourself too seriously.

Enjoy!

JEN GILLEN
proud mom of Scout

*Consider all that you have
on your mind.*

Breathe in. Breathe out.

*Now consider what Scout has to say
about whatever concerns you.*

Success is sweet.

Keep your eye
on the prize.

Life is full
of choices.
Choose wisely.

When life overwhelms you,
take a nap and find your center.

The harder you work,
the luckier you will be.

Don't luck into success.

A hat is an easy way
to be captivating.

Recognize when to loosen
up and screw around.

Introspection is an acquired skill.

Don't be
afraid to
take off
the mask—
no matter
how cool it
looks.

The power of imagination
is unlimited, use it.

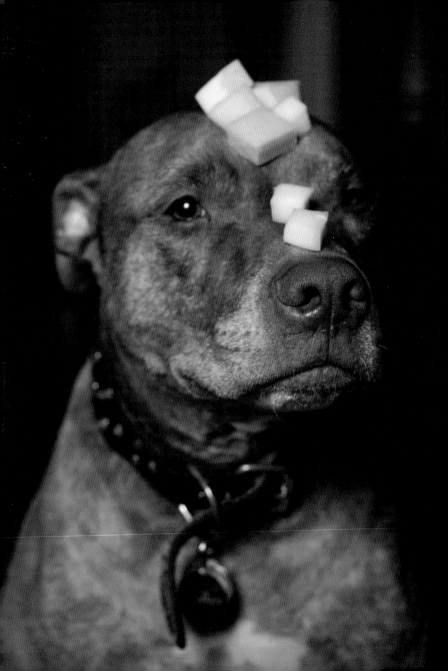

Happy people plan actions;
they don't plan results.

Don't let your
stomach rule
your mind.

Accept challenges
as they come.

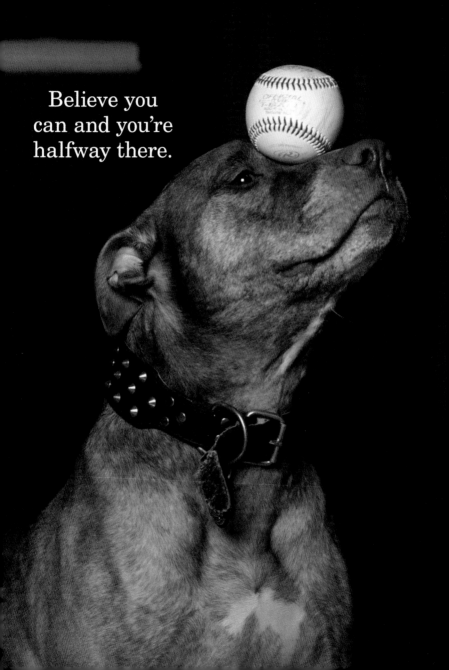

Believe you can and you're halfway there.

Confront your desires.

When it matters,
give into yourself.

Close your eyes.

Think of all your worries.

Open your eyes.

*Let Scout show you how
to let go and find your
place of peace.*

If you can't find it, stop worrying and it will appear.

Sometimes it's okay not to know what's out there.

Enemies are just people whose stories you haven't listened to.

A nice hot bath will
cure everything.

"Patience you must have." —Yoda

Prudence is
overrated.

Amid the chaos, create distractions.

If it weren't for hopes, your heart would break.

Falling is a part
of balance.

Make small changes.

Find your stillness.

Derive strength from
your softness.

You might get sick of lemonade... get used to it.

Others will judge you needlessly; take it as a challenge and prove them wrong.

Don't let the past haunt you;
live in the present.

Indulge your vices.

Don't play
games that
you can't win.

Look beyond appearances.

Laugh at yourself.

Be gentle with others.

Let Scout teach you how to accept yourself completely.

Find the support you need.

It will take the right person to bring you out of your shell.

Not everything
will fit.

Share your secret
only with the ones
you trust.

When in Rome,
do as the Romans do.

Angels come in all forms.

Service of any kind is noble.

Some days you're the rescuer;
some days you're the rescued.

Give a little…

Conversation and tea will
purify your soul.

Memories
take time
to collect.

Be eager for new adventures.

Dog with Sausages by Wilhelm Trübner (1878)

Many before you have forged
a path so that you may have
the life you have now.

Don't be a
slave to time.

Don't save your Sunday best
for Sundays only.

You are within your right to
fake it until you make it.

Be French.

Always,
make an
entrance.

"The flower of sweetest smell is shy and lowly."
—William Wordsworth

"Learning without thought is labor lost." —Confucius

Don't be full of yourself.

Celebrate yourself.

Being yourself is the best gift
you can give yourself.

The Life of Scout

Scout is a nine-year-old pit bull who likes to spend his day snoozing, snacking, and getting his ears scratched. He lives in a full household with two cat brothers and a new dog sister, who's trying to steal his thunder.

He has come a long way from the day I

saw him in the rescue center. Now, through the *Stuff on Scout's Head* blog, Scout and I work very hard not only to bring voice to the many dogs, especially pit bulls, in rescue centers waiting to be adopted and find their forever home, but also the detrimental effects of Breed Specific Legislation (BSL).

Scout lives in Ontario, where Breed Specific Legislation (BSL) is in effect. BSL is a law that restricts the ownership of certain breeds of dogs when they are perceived to be dangerous. While some think this might be an effective way of controlling dog bites and attacks, there are others, like me, who think that the law neglects a big piece of the problem, the owner. Any dog can be made vicious by an irresponsible and uncaring owner and

Scout and I work tirelessly to show how this affects all dog owners and lovers. Due to this law, Scout has to wear a muzzle in public and be kept on a leash and numerous other pit bull–type dogs are euthanized and not given a chance at being loved.

Please visit and support groups in your area who encourage responsible dog ownership and work toward mindful alternatives to Breed Specific Legislation. In his home town of London, Ontario, Scout supports and raises funds for the All Breed Canine Rescue in London, Ontario, as well as Bullies in Need.

Thank you,

JEN GILLEN & SCOUT

JEN GILLEN is Scout's owner and creator of the Tumblr blog *Stuff on Scout's Head*. She rescued Scout from an animal shelter and created the blog on a whim to showcase how patient, loyal, and gentle pit bulls can be with the right training. Now she uses the blog to draw attention and donations to various animal shelters and advocates for responsible dog ownership. Jennifer and Scout live in Toronto, Ontario. Please visit Jen and Scout on twitter at @stuffonscouts or visit stuffonscoutshead.com.

ACKNOWLEDGMENTS

Thanks to everyone who has shared a laugh along the way, and to everyone who helped make this possible; Julia for being Scout's second mom all this time; Shane for becoming part of our little family; Tina and John for guiding me on this journey; Sean and Baloni for getting the ball rolling on all of this; Sweetpea's and My Little Bike Shop for letting us invade their shops; Madi, Max, and Chris for helping me capture Scout at his most handsome; all of Scout's friends, both four-legged and two-legged; and last but not least, Scout would like to thank his agent, Yfat Reiss Gendel, and his editor, Sophia Muthuraj, for which there are no words or barks to fully appreciate what they've helped him do.

PHOTO CREDITS